Still

Also by Christopher Meredith

Poems
This
Snaring Heaven
The Meaning of Flight
Black Mountains: poems and images from the Bog~Mawnog Project
Air Histories

Fiction
Shifts
Griffri
Sidereal Time
The Book of Idiots
Brief Lives – six fictions
Please

For children
Nadolig bob Dydd
Christmas Every Day

As editor
Five Essays on Translation (with Katja Krebs)
Moment of Earth

Translation
Melog a novel by Mihangel Morgan

Still

Christopher Meredith

Seren is the book imprint of
Poetry Wales Press Ltd.
Suite 6, 4 Derwen Road, Bridgend, Wales, CF31 1LH
www.serenbooks.com
facebook.com/SerenBooks
twitter@SerenBooks

ISBN: 978-1-78172-614-3
ebook: 978-1-78172-615-0

A CIP record for this title is available from the British Library.

The publisher acknowledges the financial assistance of the Books Council of Wales.

Cover artwork: Detail from 'The Hunters in the Snow' (Winter),
1565, Pieter Breughel the Elder. © Kunsthistorisches Museum, Vienna /
incamerastock / Alamy Stock Photo.

Author website: christophermeredit9.wixsite.com/website

Printed in Bembo by Severn, Gloucester.

Contents

Moving picture   7
Still   8
Air camera   9
Standing place   10
Stereoscope   12
A strife of ants   13
John Blight at The Land's End   14
Upstairs   16
Even in dreamscapes   18

Old Spyder   21
Statues of comedians   22
Paperclips   24
Materialist   26
Clearing song   27
The train north   31
Island   33
Steampunk jungle   34
Nightfall   37
Horseshoe crabs   38

Dail poethion, Cwmorthin   43
Nettles, Cwmorthin   44
There could be temples   45
North coast swing   47

Still air:
   On Allt yr Esgair   55
   Allt spring   56
   Fumitory   57
   Village birds   58
   Ghost   62
   Ash trees   63
   Sound of leaves not falling   64
   In this stilled air the turning trees   65
   Solstice   66
   Winter woods   68

Notes   70
Acknowledgements   71

Moving picture

Memory dislikes motion –

– meaning it's some freezeframe
that persists.

In the sequence where it briefly was
it was inconsequential, unconsidered,
more for glimpse than gaze,
weightless and fugitive

and only these years later
in this synaptic conjuring
grown weighty with a fixity
it never had.

But is it more that what's disliked
is motion completed

so these people on a sunlit doorstep, say,
apprehended in a beam that fell
through the eye into the brain,
are forever swimming in that moment's
movement,
lifting a cup, moving an eye
in the action of turning away
the journey always incomplete and moving
still?

Still

At the banister above you an old man stands
in long johns like you'll never see again
except in films, backlit by an open door
smiling and lifting a slow hand

and you are forever in slow
motion sailing down the narrow stairs.
Your eyes are rolling up to watch
his head inclining gently as you go.

That's all. Rerun it. Look again. He lifts
a hand that's bossed and broad. He smiles
and pinpoints of white stubble light
the folding cheek. The moustache shifts.

No no, they say. *You never saw him.*
He couldn't stand, and you were far too young.
But you did. He could. And were you cradled
down the darkening drift, a babe in arms?

Again. That backlight is the sun. Same hand slowly
raised, same slow-inclining head, same kind smile,
his shape at the handrail this time hunched like
a passenger who's slipping from the quay

too courteous yet to turn back to the glare
of the final room, though he hungers to, and will.
Memory is the still of slow forgetting,
the black and aching decades boiled to air,

cooled to this crawling droplet in the pipe
moving still and still in this suspension
rolling on its empty convolutions
to catch and lose a world in hard white light.

Air camera

Smile, you said on the mountaintop
by the windbreak cairn we'd built
stone by scavenged stone.

Cocked thumbs and index fingers framed
the centre of your face.
A middle finger clicked
a piece of air.

That's one for my memory bank, you said

so accidentally filed it
into mine.

And was it half our lives
ago? A two-shot of the boys
standing absurdly close and stiff
with comedy smudgebox smiles
hair out sideways in the wind

and all around
the stonework of the clouds
unheaping.

Standing place

'Stanza': Italian, 'room', 'standing place'

When you step in to the empty room
you interrupt whatever it was
that the room wasn't doing

you break the calm
of the lucid glass
on a lonely lake
and it rocks
and a wave refracts across
let's say

the rug on a pinewood floor
and ruffles the solid fireplace

the table shakes

the sculpted teapot still as de Chirico
does a jelly shiver
and resets

the frozen desklamp
melts and lists

the windowglass becomes
its own blown curtain
and the garden outside billows
and settles

the sofa starts from its doze
and lifts a head and stares at
where you seem to be.

And if you're smart
you pause just one step in
and slowly lower the foot you've raised
arms out for balance
and you barely move
as you barely breathe
and you stand
try
tottering
to meet
the stillness of the pool,
become the statue in an empty square.

But you are the blurs on the street
in early photographs
the ghost in the room
the solid room that barely senses you
in this glass shudder.

This is the standing place
where you can't stay
the still lake in the dream of trees
doing still
the thing it does not do.
These are the words telling nothing
that are there before
and after you.

Stereoscope

Blade-sharp through the stereoscope
the double pictures fuse and lean
into the room: hovels crouching on a slope
of desert under hard midwestern sun –

each beaten warrior in full feather,
semi-profile, clutching a tomahawk,
scorched face gazing somewhere other,
obliging the camera with that tragic look

away in stoic or bemused connivance –
impassive children, each a stone-age Alice
composed to please a lens that can't convince
us of the *dis* it would have preface

passionate. Between record and elegy
for what's not gone the silver nitrate traps them
and appals with a somatic clarity
so you could almost touch the meaning of *dead calm.*

A dividend of conquest is this space
for creativity, plate after plate
made to deck the parlours of the curious
and hymn the peoples they'd annihilate.

A strife of ants

For that hour one September morning
the locals must have sat
up on this hill and watched,
from among trees or by their herds,
the keeneyed young perhaps describing
what they saw to the older ones –

the figures moving down there on the plain
some banners and an orchestra of pikes
their patterned dance like
starlings folding on a sky.

They must have heard some shouting, drums,
and there'd be spurts of whitish smoke
going inexplicably sideways
then slackening, yielding to the drift of air,
and a tinsel of small flashes,
the pops and cracks a little out of synch.
Perhaps, even, if the breeze was right,
they'd catch a whiff of saltpetre,
a reek of horse.

Presently hungry men would come
dirtied with earth and blood
and treat them rough and steal
their milk and eggs and ale.

But for now
the air was growing still
and promising a pleasant day
the far smoke thinning to a shred
and six hundred tiny figures lying dead
mostly. Some starlings were flying away.
Something, it seemed, had been decided.

John Blight at The Land's End

The British bards named it Penrhin Guard, "the Promontory of Blood,"
from some fearful conflict which took place there
J. T. Blight, author and illustrator, *A Week at The Land's End* (1861)

My witness was composed
in patience and a thinking eye
and then that craft and industry that graved
the shifting world into a fixity of lines.

So inland and where sea perturbed the rock
I walked and sketched to score the plates
and wrote all down, wrote it all
each anecdote each inch and history

and in my lines my own good sense and learning placed
with the layered ages and the layered land,
portraying: here, a comely inn or church,
an ancient stone (a tranquil figure in for scale);
and there, close in, a fish, a clifftop plant, a bird,
all ordered and contained, composed.

And I watched seas wash away ancestral temples
or men topple them for pigsties
and a yard of barren dirt
watched them dig for gold or tin
for their hearts' alchemy
and digging so uproot the deep stone
of their own story,
stilling what I could in steel and ink –
fishscale, oriole, club moss, cromlech,
fugitive stones and fugitive tongues

and I stood where the rock shore stands
and falls away
essayed in the same scratched plate
to remake its granite stacks and blocks
and render the unthinking tide
to move and still atlantics
in the one carved line

stood becalmed and stormracked in
my own head's land
drenched in the foam of intellectual blood
and calmly, calmly stared into
the churning chambers where
stone and ocean trade their elements
and listened calmly, calmly heard
in each surge's hiss the quenching of
a *Lyonesse* an *Ys*
and calmly hid and showed it all
yes all of it or all I could
in tight precision of the hard grooves
scarred in steel

and into those black runnels
into those torn funnels of the senseless rock
I let fall, my friends my murderers,
my own five wits
I poured them all away
I poured my wits
I poured my wits away.

Upstairs

Several lives later
before the last was cleared
I climbed the narrow stairs again.

And there were just the two rooms after all.
Long years I'd dreamed or half-remembered three –
You'd think them needful for so many dead,
crowded, in the skull,
with solving treasure packed in trunks,
on smokebloomed shelves.

Yet in the first, mean room
just long enough for lying down –
a standing crowd of zimmer frames,
her incontinence pads all packeted and stacked.
In the other, more of the same
and a plain bed unslept in these ten years
still turned down,
two frail wardrobes, bare.

Something in us builds imaginary rooms
the walls somehow exhaling truth
a rippled glass reflecting
a familial face.
And on the battlements must be a ghost,
mustn't there, with a remembered voice
articulating things unsaid
in life,
stilled deepnesses made quick and new?

Onto the dust still landing I dragged a chair
and climbed
and prised up the flimsy attic trap
and peered in
looking for stored elucidations.

But there were mantled joists.
A cranium scraped clear.

She had known a time had come
to tidy up as best you can
and turn and leave.

A chairleg creaked. Dirt furred my hand.

And I could think of nothing
but a steep path down a cliff
all rock and light and moving air
and at its end
the sea.

Even in dreamscapes

Even in dreamscapes Breughel understood
the movement of the real north

how the inimical gorgeous cold
is always coming or just gone or here.

Hunching figures lurch and pass
a gusting fire in the black-legged woods.

Barking and the stink of breath are coiled
in the polyphony of canine tails.

One magpie's signing her brief shape
across the air of solstice grey.

And then that single upright crow
on the bough of a decorous framing tree

real as any you've ever seen
nails it, is both of this world and peeping in

as are we, but spells out how
we never can escape the frame

and is still, and stiller than
we'll ever be.

Old Spyder

Under jewelled Aldebaran
old Spyder sat, his head hunched down.

All matter he thought's just a flower fight
and all that we think heavy light

and all that's truly light seems dark
and all that's truly play seems work.

Oh we could shine such a jewelled light
but for the memory's grip on hurt
and the interference of the heart.

Statues of comedians

It's the destiny of some to be this dead.
Certain politicians, poets, murderers on stallions
or on columns become the bronze or stone too well.
If – and god forbid – civic sculpture was my trip
I'd take on some old bastard with battalions
every time ahead of saints with worthy precepts.
Metal's more appropriate to some grand malignity
like – okay let's go for it – a Thatcher.
I'd sink the Belgrano of that vicious dignity
with a tin and copper alloy cast torpedo. Gotcha!
Let them be so frozen and armorial
since utter wasness always was their aim –
to essay tin-godhood as they did's to wish such fame
as makes you nothing but your own memorial.

At first glance comedians seem little better.
After all, they choose a look to wear,
strike self-conscious attitudes on rostrums
and perhaps a few could outblair Blair,
making of their egos mausoleums.
But mostly the accoutrements are worn
for what they are.
The hat and stick are tat and flimsy shtick
we somehow cherish and discard in one.
Their oeuvres are built of vanishings
that briefly ape our frailties and vanities
in high sentence done with bungled grandeur,
in honed non sequiturs and well-turned inanities,
in spoons and jars, in Laurel's siphoned wine,
in balletic teeterings on catastrophic borders,
in drunk Frank Randle walking up some stairs,
in all the right notes, sunshine,
necessarily not in the right order.
Their whole careers are
just seconds of vibrating air.

So if I cared enough I'd groan
at these well-meant commissioned makings.
O, Ocean, wash away that desperate lone man
not quite dancing on the beach in Morecambe.
And poor Cooper cast in bronze comes stalking
out of nightmare scarier than Mary's monster-
patchwork of the grave. The fez is almost
Boris Karloff's flattened head, the mad grin
modelled in frozen dung's a rictus
that only makes him look dead
scared. If I cared I would fix a metaphor
about the everything that's lost along with wax.
Oh, the graft, the waste of days, the skill misspent
to kill the laugh bronze dead and miss the point.

Paperclips

For Leigh Hendra on her birthday

1

Minimal spring
ultimate Bauhaus chair
unsittable upon
in unupholstered chrome.

2

In French:
trombones!
Think Charles Trenet
think that accent
wet and trilling on the   *trrr*
blowing a kiss to the   *omb*
And to follow
    the mellowing
essless embouchure
pouting its gong in   *one(s)*.
But, ah, those Gallic ironists –
there's no mouthpiece and no bell.
These trombones are Trappists.
Their slide is noiseless.
Muted in angular selfinvolvement
they keep that tight steel circuit
closed on silence.
The habit of these clips is
unspeaking ellipsis.

3

But some have that minimal lifted lip
angled to take the sliding sheet
as if about to speak
but thinking better of it.
This is the wellmannered clip.

4

Some fold arms and lie flat.
They must be coaxed to open.
The outer loop longing forever
to resheathe the inner
they yearn to return to the
plane of themselves.

But oh, the paperwork,
one this side of the sheet
the other the other
though it's hardly chaste
as they press and they press
and they're Cathy from Wuthering
and each is a ghost
making love to the other
from beyond a veil
and whatever the letter the script or the tract is
the chromiumplated high tensile fact is
they'll always be one.

5

On the whitening page they're heaped
like skis
and these are the vanishing tracks of the travellers gone
somewhere far off, warm.

Materialist

I made the ink
that makes this mark
from the worm of a wasp
and the grief of an oak

and I blackened the blood
that writes the word
with the rust that sheared
the anchor cord

and I thickened the ink
that loads the pen
with the tears of a tree
that laughed in the sun.

If a poem is light
and a poem is dark
it's bred of the ink
that makes the mark.

If a word is life
and a word is death
it's bred in the blood
that comes of earth.

Clearing song

After their leaving
I called out: No more.
I tore down the curtain,
flung open the door

I chucked the old sofa
out into the street
and snatched my own carpet
from under my feet.

And when I was upright
I scanned my own shelves.
They were crowded with intricate
ghosts of dead selves

and crystalline memories
in out-of-date jars,
the breath of dead lovers,
the dust of dead stars.

And I paused, and I kissed them
and put them aside,
for my gift is the present
and I am his bride.

I dissolved all my sorrows
into a white pot
and whirled in a paintbrush
and whitened the lot –

I who paint pictures
and stitched the kids' toys,
who embroidered my garden
with polychrome joys,

I who weave music
with fiddle and bow –
I painted a whiteness
as silent as snow

on each cornice and ceiling
each floor and each frame
and said: Let a new tenant
now write her name

and bottle her memories
on the white shelves
and clutter the cupboards
with ghosts of dead selves.

Let historians scratch for
who slept in which room.
My gift is the present
and he is my groom.

And in the last cupboard
was one mystery –
I found all my yearning
forged into a key.

It was worked in black iron
as long as my hand.
Its bit was rust-furrowed
and grained like the sand,

its lean shank was true as
the mast of a ship
and its lug like a tiller
was warm in my grip.

I weighed its calm anchor
against all my rush.
In left hand I clutched it,
in right hand, the brush.

And when all was whitened
and emptied and swept
I cast off my fever
and lay down and slept

becalmed on the white floor
as smooth as a sea,
dreaming the palace
that fitted the key.

It was figured with carvings
and tinted with paints
and alive with the spirits
of makers and saints.

In girlhood I'd glimpsed it
and it sang to me.
Now the ghost of its whisper
was sound in the key.

Its gables were rhythm
its gardens were rhyme
and its floors and its landings
were layered like time

and I lived in its music
with eyelids shut tight,
and when I awakened,
an ocean of light

made a pale aching silence
across the bare room.
And this was the present
and he was my groom.

There's a field that I've heard of
in woods to the west.
There I will journey
with key on my breast

hung like a talisman,
and among the lithe trees
I'll pitch my pavilion
wherever I please.

The frame of sweet timber
I'll fell and I'll pare,
the walls will be fabric
that dances in air

that I'll work from the bright threads
I'll weave on the loom
of my bow and my fiddle
to colour the room.

I'll stitch my new garden
with jewels of light
and watch the live galaxies
whirl through the night.

So at anchor I'll voyage
the late years in the west
and find rest in renewal
renewal in rest.

The train north

Yes we should have got one going back
one of those endless engines pouring from the north
hauling shaved trunks stacked up like the dead
in wagon after wagon southward to the fires
we should have caught an empty going back
a flareskirted steel machine its firebox a forge
and gone north
with the furthest ticket we could get
away from that mid region where
an almost gentle autumn closed
its twilight fist on us
where snow fell among the fall of leaves
away from closely argued seminars
from the ticking crossways
and the dim bright happy bars
huddled in consolatory songs
and in that Special with no driver and no lights
at a rhythmic window we'd have watched
the treefletched dark horizon vanish into dark
and passed the lit white splashes of deserted towns
the lonely drunks in chainwheeled cars
slewing circuits on the footthick ice
in rosaries of diesel smoke
and crossed the felled dark plains and watched
the draped electric green aurorae
glimmer over frozen lakes and drop behind
and slipped from dark to stone black pressing on the brain
till even the smear the memory trace
of fire and light from the vanished south
would have vanished from the candles in our eyes
and on to the solid sea beyond the towns
that imitate the sky and ice in scratching
sk sk like steel studs on a granite road
and over we would have gone
over the hurling curve of the Arctic
slung from the limb of the world
the rails and the sleepers falling from us
and on into heat death into solid space
where the states of matter slacken borders

between air and earth and sea and tongues
and we would have been transfigured with them
into something black and crystalline
beyond that isogloss where all is one and zero
where ice is a syllable each syllable is ice
so each breath like iron in the trough
would have quenched on air and hissed and gasped
yes   ice   jää   ia

Island

In parched night on an island once
  I saw on a ridge across a bay
    a forest flower into flame
      that dazzled on the rising sea

and the wildfire cooled to an ochre moon
  that whitening swam into the sky
    and the island sank into dark and calm
      forgetting its minute of prophecy

Steampunk jungle

Cwmtawe 2017

That hot day
when the ridge in perpetual shade
even that ridge bulging above us
sweated and steamed
we walked you and I through
the hot mash in darkness
where they ripped up the railtrack
and the river was sunstruck
and brown through the trees
and the streams off the mountain
the paths and the ditches
were black with dead waters
and huge beeches and oak dug
their toes in the black scree
that urged them to slide and
to topple and crush us
we walked you and I in
the drowning forest
in the lattice of darkness
and splashes of sunlight
that lasered the canopy
and *look* you said *look the marsh orchids*
and mechanical as lampposts
they lit up the walkway
to that branchtangled shrine
in the steampunk jungle
a gibbet with pit boots
a pit lamp and battery
a hard hat on a post like
a skull in a story
dead flowers old snapshots
and felt pen endearments
this makeshift memorial
to those four last miners
maybe the very last
to drown in these mountains
in black mud and stone

and we passed fallen tunnels
like broken gods gaping
smashed chapels of engines
in ivy lianas
and amid the racked forest
a pylon surged upward
out of the bramble
the fern and the knotweed
and mineral grew scaly
and xylem and girder
and soared overhead in the
palæozoicoanthropocene
and *look* you said *look*
and there in the rust rills
that ran from the mountain
among roots and rail ends *look*
and there was the cracked cog
of some great machine
and with mud rusty fingers
we hauled it from water
the massy half disc of it
hand thick and fluted
precise notches locking
on sweating air
and we carried it down to
the still living river
and washed it where alder tongues
lapped at the water
we washed it this relic
this fragment of hubris
and didn't know then there
was no hand that made it
this fibre made iron
this fern from the hot swamps
from the ages when sweet air
bred marvels and giants
and oh my dead fathers
my burning earth's children
who forced me to witness
it never was crushed to
the carbon that killed us

and we didn't know then
it would wither in sunlight
and crumble to nothing
this tree before time
and over the drumrush
where river beat boulders
we heard the mad traffic
still roaring for murder
and a pterosaur heron
wheeled over the river
and a dipper too beaten
for flying or diving
fell down to a rock in
the seething brown waters
and spreading the cross
of herself on the stone
she grew still

Nightfall

Light cools
  on the hill above the villages.
The shadowline
  is flowing up the field.
See the wounded
  limping from the ridges
with rags tied
    round the remnant of a world.
They watch
  the houses' gradual effacement
under the shadow
  as each light goes out.
The villagers
  are shuttering the casements
and call
    for barricades across the street.

In cities
  in each bright glass-fronted tower
the chief beast squats
  adorned with human love
proclaiming
  that the sorrows will be fewer
if we close up
  the gates and so disprove
the wounded
    who yet march towards the threshold
with burning rags
    to set alight the world.

Horseshoe crabs

Under planished clouds
on the dusk quiet road
we passed picket and flags
and calm pastel clapboard
gone glassy in stormlight
and over the wall to the sea

and the steel sea was folding
and beating its swordblade
on shingle that roared like
the falling of money
the deafness of factories
in profligate making

the heaped shields of horseshoes
a flung dune along it
their half mile a rampart
of slimelacquered bronzes
pigtailed and intricate
each disc a warrior

forged in cold oceans
of hammered millennia
armoured for suffering
this day's attrition
surging in waters
as if they were fallen.

But turn a corpse over
lift the ribbed helmet.
Instead of the pulped brain
clawed hands are tending
the soft bench of a mouth.
The armoured tail flexes.

Its life reeks of rotting.
And it roared in our ears,
the sensekilling ocean
the grating of bodies
in commerce in warfare
in stormhurled amplexus

with no *was* and no *will be*.
Language is matchwood.
The strange world will enter
paleblooded, eyejewelled.
It stares and tells nothing
and goes nowhere but here.

Dail poethion, Cwmorthin

Ger murddun tŷ'r rheolwr
fe safant yn gôr
dan gorongylchoedd euraidd
heulwen hafau byr

a chanu maent
yn ddi-sain, heb arweinydd,
i'r cartrefi chwâl,
i wyneb dedwydd y llyn uchel:

Lle cynt bu rhwygo gewyn
ymgrymwn yn ein cân
ein hadau yn alawon
lle'r aeth eich hoelion trwm
yn groch ar graig

a gwatwar yw ein hemyn
ein gwên yn weiren bigog,
pob cytgan yn ei dymor
yn dychwelyd
yn ysgafndroed, yn gryf,
yn chwerthin

ac mae trymder eich ymdrechion yn ddim
ond sibrwd rwbel yn y nos
dim ond mudandod y gwefusau tyn
ym meini nadd y muriau
heb do, heb drigolion

a phob blwyddyn codwn floedd
ein buddugoliaeth, ein bodoli,
ninnau'r blodau cyfrwys,
gan dagu'r pyrth o grawiau
lle'r aethoch chi.

Nettles, Cwmorthin

Outside the ruin of Tŷ'r Manijar
they lean tall as men
sedate and dusted in brief sunlight
singing a noiseless air
to the broken houses,
to the high lake:

We stand where once you cracked your sinews
spring bad flowers
where your boots scraped rock

and oh, the heaviness of all your effort
whispers only in the slide of rubble
in capless walls packed Aztec tight,
unpeopled

and yes, this song's an irony
a kind of laughing,
each chorus in its season coming back
and always strong and light
and taunting.

With no more effort than it takes to be
ourselves
we make each year our feather shape in air,
us subtle flowers armoured in ground glass,
singing in the wake of all your striving,
choking the stone gates where
your children passed.

There could be temples

Llandudno Pier, August 2014

You run the gauntlet of *Amusement*
through a narrow souk of shouting stalls
– *Water Gun Gallery Just £3.50!*
No Photographs in Hats Until

You've Paid... and somewhere under the cliff face
of the Grand Hotel where
the scrolled rust of an iron staircase ends
like an accident, mid air -

somewhere there you cross the border
and, as if smoke cleared,
as if you were through the back of the wardrobe,
you step from tarmac onto boards

and this seems open water, sudden calm.

The long perspective of the boardwalk points to sea.
Buttressed with chinoiserie pavilions
it fixes stillness in a symmetry

that lets you sense,
beneath the slats beneath your feet,
mute music of the green sea working.

Souk runners stroll now, quietly,
breathing at ease as if a struggle's over,
dissipated in its own success.

The man in shorts, the woman in gold sandals
stand frozen at the rail
under the rock wave frozen in the Orme

and even the nippers can't break the spell
pelting towards that last pagoda
up the timber arrowshaft that's aimed

so purposeful, stock still, beyond the water.
    And who are you, after all, to find this wanting,
that under the final cupola's pale spelter

instead of a Buddha stands a bright kiosk
holding out the offering of *Change*
or that against each angled wall

as in a chapter house the obelisks
of one-armed bandits blink, and have no arms at all,
and wait unchanging for your ghost oblation?

North coast swing

1

It's mild, no wind, and late sun rubs a pearl
through pastel cloud above the war memorial.
Between the shallow crescent of well-kept hotels
– Riverdale, Saint Kilda's, Brig-y-Don –
and the artificial shingle shore
they dumped to keep the sea at bay,
its back towards the waves, the swing band all in black

unclips its cases, tests the valves, unpacks
the girderwork of seats and music stands.
The seafront benches fill, the deckchairs gape
and the leader – white tie, black shirt, sleeked hair
ashy as the gentle sea – begins to time.
After the dead slow patter he turns
to face the band, the tide, and, routinely,

wags the stick. Count Basie it was, apparently,
who sang The Body Electric.
Mobility scooters, batteries whirring,
slow down to watch, and could make of it
a two tone joke that's off the beat, but
in fact they're pretty good, the shy band
etched against the sea. The dolorous

trumpet's muted as the colours
and it's nice that way. The crowd, mute too,
is palely curious. We don't know what to feel
except to feel that we don't know,
or know maybe that though this isn't an event
it's willing to be more than another act
of waiting in the place called Holiday.

2

Anyway, these timorous-smooth renditions
half ease us some where, some time other,
rubbing a cuff on a misted pane
till we can see, a little blurred,
how the leader's cormorant shape
's picked out elemental and absurd on cloud
or how that Trajan's column of ads

descanting on memorial
stands like a sample core drilled out of time,
the limp not limpid record of an age
as dreamed by Denmark Street and Radio Fun.
So, Jurassic-deep a withered poster calls
Remember The Times! A Good Ol'
1940s Knees Up! (Cast Of Eight)

and in a newer layer, Jimmy Osmond,
late career, huge-headed in a titch cartoon,
steps into Mickey Rooney's panto shoes,
then some am-drams doing bits from Brigadoon,
and closest to today's the seventies Motown Tribute
with Venue Cymru's guest band, The Detroits.
Let's hear it for those myth-frail cities burning gas!

For the abandoned too? For Kilda, say, Cwmorthin?
Somewhere eastward out of earshot the roads
are roaring still. Behind our backs unseen
the fractured centuries of this country press
in the raindrenched mass of farms and rock.
And we are not quite idling here, in neutral
tones, at the edge of something, mumbling song.

3

Not long now. The Body Electric,
via Pennsylvania, leads to a String of Pearls
that slip by the ear, translucent, cool
as the conductor's tie. He eyes his watch
then warily eyes us and turns away
for One More Time to lead the wave, to lead the tide,
to lead the pearly sky. Beyond

the blank mechanics of the band he sees
the nuances of grey stretch out immense, unhuman
into the toppled corridor of air
that rifts the sea and cloud.
Pale jazzhands of the windfarms drift
milling small change from the fitful breeze
as if a hundred clocks were running down

and almost at the weld of sky and sea
a gas rig, never quite in time,
snaps out a neon flag of yellow flame.
And still. In the dead air pause,
his baton down, before the soft rain of applause
he hears the waters sigh against the rock
the shingle shift.

Still air

On Allt yr Esgair

Under the serpent galaxy
   the motifs of stone hills recur
in scoops and curls across the sky
    cutting the landscape's signature.

Under the rhythms of the name
   the coiling water of the Usk
inscribes red rock and combs red clay
    with a gleaming mercury arabesque.

And the larval micromoth
   inside the thickness of a leaf
mines a tunnel with her mouth
    to carve a curious hieroglyph.

What else is left for us but this?
   With pen and brush to shape our track,
like moths and streams and hills and stars,
    a human shadow on the rock.

Allt spring

The felled wood's stiller than the lake
death stiff in its bark
each toppled tree
and the flame of a robin ignites the brake
with birthsong and an elegy

Fumitory

The names are marvellous treachery:
mwg y ddaear
fumeterre
fumitory.
So what if they remember
some dead rite of burning,
some propitiatory cleansing?
Smoke is just a blur,
an ending.

No. Intricate fumitory is
a kind of opposite of smoke.
In these lines and frettings
mud weaves
tongues of petals that can sing
precision, counterpointing fractals
in a fugue of leaves,
condensing
earth to air,
to music.

Village birds

Villages are communities of birds as well as of people – William Condry

1

You landtrapped monsters
must be watched.

Sometimes you try with brutal energy
to rear into the third dimension

on heaps of stones
or with strange wings of fire.

The effort leaves you spent
your flat world waste.

We keep an eye and, most times, keep
a beat ahead

because you purblind
cousins of the worm

can't as we do see,
say, the quickness of a fish through water

or calculate the light's refraction,
can't feel through your oozy hides

the calms and freshes
of the liquid sky.

2

What blurry intimations we must seem
glimmering with the stars and moon

through the ocean over you
then sudden visitants

too quick in flashes of precision
what was remote as dream

remade in meteor storms
of swifts' black syncopation.

3

We bring meaning
to your heapings of the curious rocks.

Those chimneys are evolved
for purging jackdaws' ticks.

The privet rooms are meant for us.
We hold our councils on your walls

notate on staves you draw with wires
polyphonies you'll never hear

and play their concert
in a hall of winds.

4

So you spread offerings for
your half-seen gods.

Sometimes, with bobbing circumspection,
we accept.

If we as you had words and gods
perhaps we'd worship you

as you also pray before
the creatures that you eat.

We might then, even, pity
bottom-dwellers crawling in mud roads.

But we don't.
We didn't ask your suffering

for us whose miles-deep parish is
the teeming air.

Ghost

And once in late summer,
  the cool ridge grown dark
    under bloodmarbled sundown

from fern surge and gorse drift
  its cries patching silence
  came one low voice chiming

in still air and stirred air
  conversing with absence
  alone on a sapling

unmoving unceasing
  and paler than frost smoke
  the mistle ghost singing

Ash trees

Each of these feathered ash trees is
a slut,
a rake.
Come October's party they're the first
to let the yellow music take
them to the floor to dance
a trembling striptease.

Don't think
this is some last hurrah –
its wanton and demure abundance is
a promise
with a wink
of what's to come.
They get into the swing.
The mood's hypnotic
and the air's a drug
and see how musc
ular,
they are,
the last veil gone, at ease.

At the party's end in next year's dawn all starts.
They'll arch
their trunks and yawn
and leaning to the floral rug,
throw down their keys.

Sound of leaves not falling

Out of unmoving air
a handful of the millions
fell.

You held your breath
and tried to hear
what stirred them.

Nothing.

Then the bloodlit panes
not falling
tinked and clicked in
choral
sighing
and became the cipher of the unheard
world

holding
still
the tune
of the about-to-be

like rain
beginning.

In this stilled air the turning trees

In this stilled air
   the turning trees
        it seems are waiting.

Even the birch that flickered tinsel
even the nervy feathers of ash
 hang still
   and all the woodland has become
the picture of its own slow patience.

Not that the music's stopped.
In sap that's slowing
     under bark
obedient to the
     tilt of earth
in leaves that microfractionally curl
the tiny modulations
   still must work

     but the orchestra's so close to mute
the submerged beat so slowed
it takes you to the edge of sense
where sound and memory and self dispute
           identities
   before some new crescendo to
a haemorrhage can come

and you know your own blood's whisper
 - *lob* it says, and *dub* it says -
   is the whisper of the world

  and still it stands
  and still, as Galileo almost said, it moves
this music of the shape we make in time
the almost
   stillness of the air
we have to play.

Solstice

The woods in snow
   are a pillared room
      where all is chill
         and all is warm

      and whitegowned music
            paces in
   a step and a step
      so statelily

and her tread
like a strobelight
stills the air
in a sombre
   December
      minor key

      bird minims climb
         the invisible stair
   that winds in the
   ghostpale winter air

and under the whitening
               darkening hill
         music paces
            paces
                     still

and snowflakes swarming
                     coalesce
   to make of all
            one nothingness

         and music still
            must tread must tread
   brow chapleted dark green and red

and in her measure
dream the seed
of the drumbeat sleeping
in the blood

and from the sleeping air
she wakes
the contrapuntal
paradox

how all's turmoil
all is calm
and all
is cool
and all is warm

and sings of how
the ice must burn
the cold sun stand
the cold sun turn

Winter woods

The alchemy of snow
        by now is understood
        how miles up it's conjured
      from drenched air
          and specks of earth that whirl
in icy vortices and grows
      ice crystals finialled like
      the ideograms of stars
that coalesce
        about the specks
   and linking ray to starry spike they
     pattern the gravid void like
          free fallers clasping hands
and whirling grey and whitening
         begin
   to feather, copter,
        this gathering
     of crystal fallers,
rock and float, slide, sideslip,
  tumble, float again
        ride down the zigzag
seesaws of the half-sustaining air

and an age
   a moment later
     enter
       the bare
   strangeness of the upper trees
   their narrow black beginnings
joining downward into deltas traced
        towards the source,
         the flood
      of blackened wood uprushing
into light
          and they brush,
    the fallers,
   by the garish softnesses of moss on trunks
    and still

they fall
            until at last they
        settle their wafer
on the tongue of earth

and we upturned can see their tiny darknesses
        whirling from pale lilac air
transform to white
    and never felt till now the thirst
we always had to know their dissolution
in the warmth of blood
against our face.

Was there ever a lousier metaphor
                        for death?
Its themes are starlight, mud and ice and sky.
 It makes a living sculpture of our breath.
    The cold catch in the throat says we're alive.

Notes

'Moving picture' – the epigraph is from John Banville's novel *The Sea*.

'John Blight at The Land's End'. J.T. Blight (1835-1911) was author and illustrator of *A Week at The Land's End* (1861), a meticulous description of the tip of his native Cornwall, detailing its land- and seascapes, flora and fauna, architecture, prehistoric remains, and including parts of its history and folklore. Blight spent the last forty years of his life in Bodmin Asylum.

'Standing place' partly arose out of a discussion with Cathy Dreyer. It was the last thing I discussed with Anne Cluysenaar before her tragic death, and is in her memory.

'The train north'. I never took the chance to travel as far north as I could when I stayed in central Finland. The Finnish and Welsh words for 'ice' are almost identical.

'Still air'. These poems grew from a project with artist and printmaker Sara Philpott. We each responded to landscapes around where we lived, I to places including Allt yr Esgair near Brecon and Philpott to places around Newtown, and exchanged ideas and work in progress. We at first intended working with William Condry's great *Natural History of Wales* but this was left behind as the work developed. His influence remains in the poems, especially in 'Village birds' and its epigraph.

Acknowledgements

Some of these poems have appeared in *Agenda, Envoi, The Lonely Crowd, Planet, Poetry Wales, Scintilla, At Time's Edge* edited by Fiona Owen, and *The Slate Sea* edited by Paul Henry. Thanks to Nicola Bickerton for asking me to write something for Leigh Hendra's birthday. I'm grateful to The Camden Trust for commissioning the pieces for *The Slate Sea*. Some of the *Still air* poems first appeared in a hand-printed booklet in an edition of fifty copies by Sara Philpott, along with her linocuts.

My thanks to the Hawthornden Trust for the award of a Fellowship in February – March 2020, when some of these poems were written.